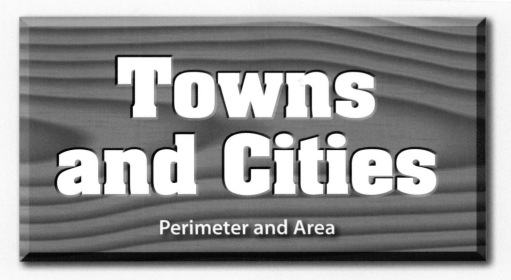

Towns and Cities

Perimeter and Area

Dianne Irving

Publishing Credits

Editor
Sara Johnson

Editorial Director
Dona Herweck Rice

Editor-in-Chief
Sharon Coan, M.S.Ed.

Creative Director
Lee Aucoin

Publisher
Rachelle Cracchiolo, M.S.Ed.

Image Credits

The author and publisher would like to gratefully credit or acknowledge the following for permission to reproduce copyright material: cover Shutterstock; p.1 iStock; pp.4–7, 9 Shutterstock; p.10 Getty Images; pp.12–13, 14 (top left) Shutterstock; p.14 (bottom right) Photolibrary.com/Alamy; p.15 iStock; p.16 Shutterstock; p.17 Corbis; p.18 Shutterstock; p.19 Photolibrary.com/Alamy; pp.20–22 Shutterstock; p.23 Getty Images; pp. 24–25 Shutterstock; p. 26 Corbis; p.27 Photolibrary.com

Diagrams by Colby Heppéll

While every care has been taken to trace and acknowledge copyright, the publishers tender their apologies for any accidental infringement where copyright has proved untraceable. They would be pleased to come to a suitable arrangement with the rightful owner in each case.

Teacher Created Materials

5301 Oceanus Drive
Huntington Beach, CA 92649-1030
http://www.tcmpub.com
ISBN 978-0-7439-0917-4
© 2009 Teacher Created Materials Publishing

Table of Contents

Settling Down

Towns and cities began when people started to live in **permanent** (PUR-muh-nuhnt) settlements. This was more than 10,000 years ago. Today, many people live in towns and cities.

Governments provide services. They make rules for how towns and cities should grow or change. These rules set **standards** about how things should be built.

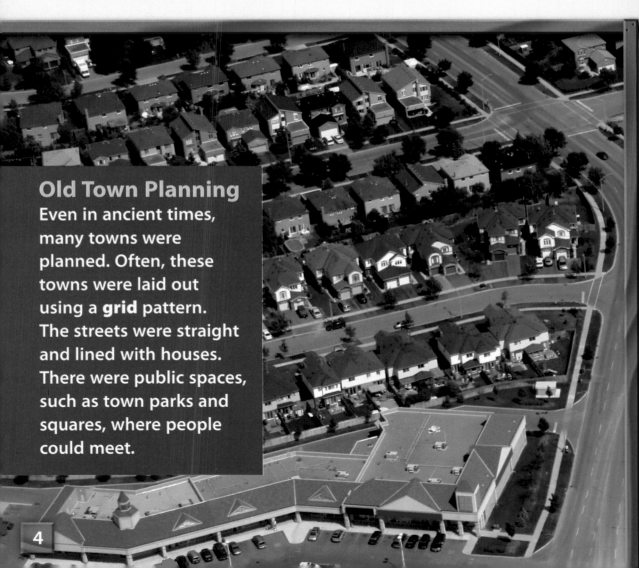

Old Town Planning

Even in ancient times, many towns were planned. Often, these towns were laid out using a **grid** pattern. The streets were straight and lined with houses. There were public spaces, such as town parks and squares, where people could meet.

The city of New York is home to more than 8 million people.

One hundred years ago, the **area** of Smalltown was 1 mile × 1 mile, or 1 square mile (1 mi.²). This means that the space inside Smalltown was 1 square mile. The **perimeter** of the town was 1 mile + 1 mile + 1 mile + 1 mile, or 4 miles. This means that the distance around Smalltown was 4 miles.

Over time, Smalltown grew bigger in size. Its **dimensions** changed. Fifty years ago, Smalltown was 2 miles long and 2 miles wide.

a. What were its area and perimeter?

Twenty-five years ago, Smalltown was 3 miles long and 2 miles wide.

b. What were its area and perimeter?

Today, the area of Smalltown is 9 square miles. Only the width of the town has changed.

c. What is the perimeter of Smalltown today?

Towns and Cities Today

Cities today may be very crowded. So, many people live in the **suburbs**. Highways are built to take people from their homes in the suburbs to the cities.

A busy highway in Beijing, China

City Populations

City	2006	2004	2000
Beijing, China	15,810,000	14,900,000	13,819,000
Seoul, South Korea	10,352,202	10,288,000	9,980,000
New York City, U.S.A.	8,214,426	8,178,201	8,018,350
Sydney, Australia	4,284,400	4,245,900	4,085,600
Los Angeles, U.S.A.	3,849,378	3,837,490	3,705,060

Sources: Beijing Municipal Bureau of Statistics; Seoul Metropolitan Government; U.S. Census; Australian Bureau of Statistics.

Sometimes, whole new suburbs are created beyond the original suburbs. These may be quite far from the city. They have schools, parks, factories, offices, and shopping malls. Each of the buildings in these new suburbs is carefully planned and measured.

LET'S EXPLORE MATH

Two suburbs lie next to each other. Both suburbs have rectangular shapes. Surrey Hills is 14 miles long and 8 miles wide. Richmond has an area of 45 square miles.

a. What is the area and perimeter of Surrey Hills?

b. What could be the length and width of Richmond?
   Hint: There may be more than one answer.

Building Houses

An area of land that is used for building new houses is called a **tract**. Town planners must decide if new roads and bus routes need to be built near new tracts. A tract is divided into sections called lots. A developer may build houses on the lots for people to buy. Or a family may buy a lot in a tract and work with an **architect** (AR-ki-tekt) to make plans for a house to be built there.

This architect helps this family plan what their house will look like.

The architect designs the house. The architect must think about the size and shape of the lot. The architect decides the best place on the lot to put the house.

Usually, a house is put in the middle of the lot. This means there is a backyard and a front yard.

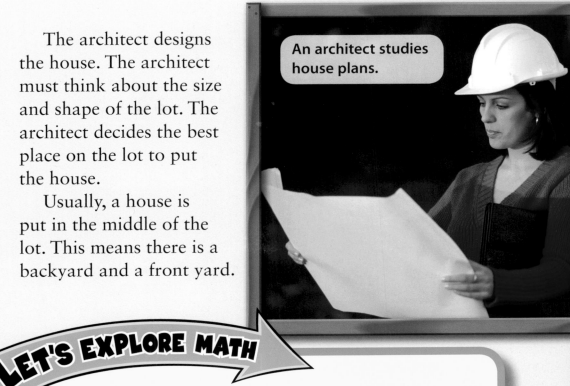

An architect studies house plans.

LET'S EXPLORE MATH

A new tract is being planned. Each lot is a rectangle. Look at the table below to find the length and width of each lot. Then redraw the table, adding 2 columns. Label the columns "Area" and "Perimeter." Fill in the information when you answer the questions below.

Lot	Length	Width
A	120 ft.	50 ft.
B	120 ft.	70 ft.
C	120 ft.	65 ft.
D	120 ft.	55 ft.

a. What is the area of each lot?

b. What is the perimeter of each lot?

c. Describe another way to figure out the perimeter of each lot.

The architect needs to know the perimeter and area of the lot. The perimeter is the distance around the lot. The area is the amount of space inside the lot. A **surveyor** (ser-VEY-er) uses a special instrument to measure the lot. The architect then uses this information to create house plans.

A surveyor using an automatic level to take measurements of a lot

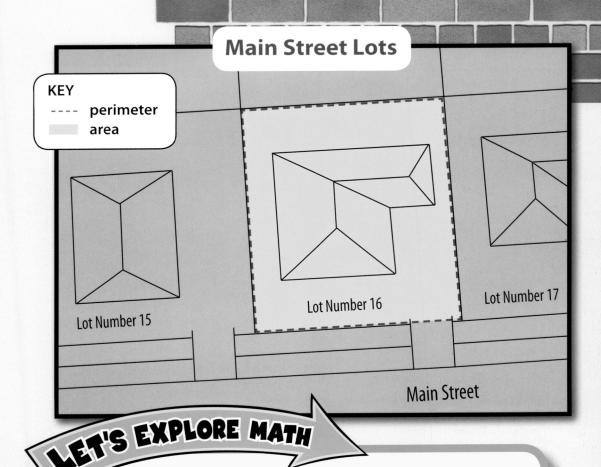

Main Street Lots

KEY
- - - - perimeter
▭ area

Lot Number 15

Lot Number 16

Lot Number 17

Main Street

LET'S EXPLORE MATH

The formula to find the area of a rectangle is:
Area of a rectangle = base × height

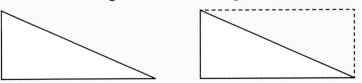

A triangle is half a rectangle. So, the formula to find the area of a triangle is:

Area of triangle = $\frac{1}{2}$ (base × height)

If the base of a triangle is 80 feet and the height is 50 feet, what is the area?

Most lots of land are rectangles, but some are **irregular** shapes. To measure the area of an irregular shape, it needs to be divided into regular shapes, such as rectangles or squares. The areas of these shapes are added together to get the area of the whole lot.

A Yard Plan

Landscape gardeners draw up plans that show where plants, trees, and paths will go.

LET'S EXPLORE MATH

These house lots are irregular shapes. Divide the lots into regular shapes and figure out the area of each lot.

a.
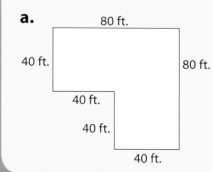

80 ft.

40 ft.

80 ft.

40 ft.

40 ft.

40 ft.

b.
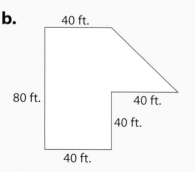

40 ft.

80 ft.

40 ft.

40 ft.

40 ft.

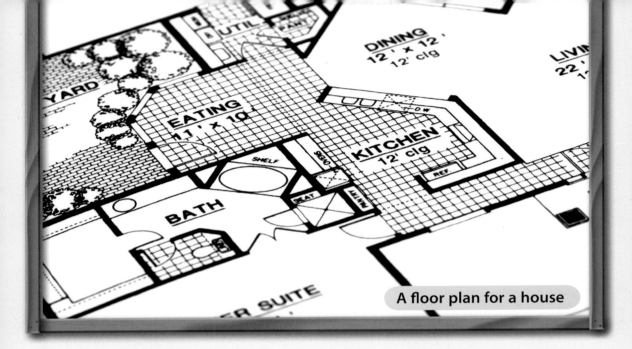

A floor plan for a house

The floor plan for a house shows the measurements of the whole house. It also shows the measurements of each room. The floor plan gives an idea of how the rooms fit together and how big they are. It shows where the doors and windows will be.

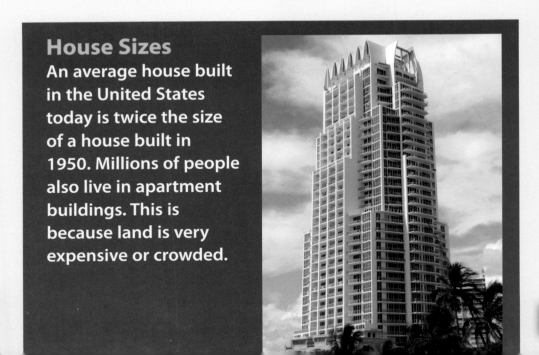

House Sizes

An average house built in the United States today is twice the size of a house built in 1950. Millions of people also live in apartment buildings. This is because land is very expensive or crowded.

Building Materials

Outside Materials

The measurements for the house need to be **accurate** (AK-yer-it). That way, the builder will buy the right amount of building materials.

For example, there are about 5 bricks for 1 square foot (0.9 m²) of wall. First, the builder figures out the area of the wall in square feet. Then the builder multiplies that number by 5. The builder will need to allow for the windows and doors. These will reduce the number of bricks needed.

A painter needs to know the area of the walls in each room that will have paint. One gallon (3.8 L) of paint is enough for about 400 square feet (37 m²) of wall.

LET'S EXPLORE MATH

A builder is building the outside wall of a house. The rectangular wall is 14 feet long and 12 feet high. The builder needs 5 bricks for each square foot of wall.

a. What is the area of the wall?

b. How many bricks are needed to build the wall?

c. One gallon of paint covers about 400 square feet of wall. Write and solve a problem about how much paint to buy.

Building Pools

Many towns have public swimming pools for the local people to use. It is important for a town to have a swimming pool because people need somewhere to learn how to swim. Most people do not have the money or space needed to build a pool at home.

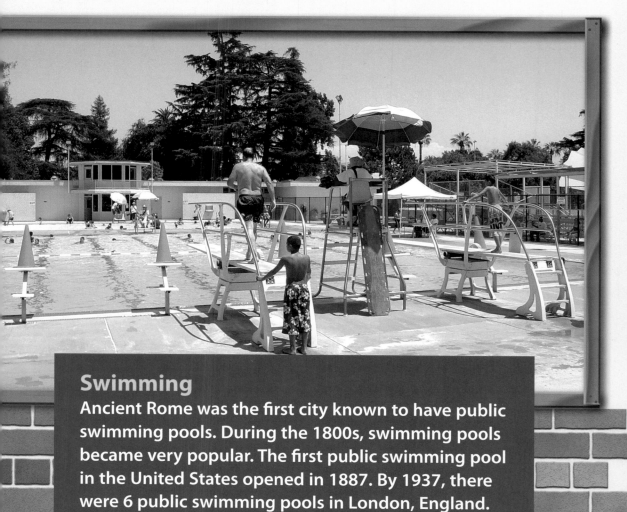

Swimming

Ancient Rome was the first city known to have public swimming pools. During the 1800s, swimming pools became very popular. The first public swimming pool in the United States opened in 1887. By 1937, there were 6 public swimming pools in London, England.

In the United States, the most popular length for a public swimming pool is 25 yards (23 m). There are 6 or 8 lanes in the pool. Each lane is 7 or 8 feet (2 or 2.5 m) wide.

Olympic pools are specially designed for **competitive** (kuhm-PET-i-tiv) swimming. They are shaped like rectangles. They must be 164 feet (50 m) long and 82 feet (25 m) wide. They must have 8 lanes and they must be at least 6.5 feet (2 m) deep.

An Olympic-sized swimming pool

There are rules for building public swimming pools. These rules are important for keeping people safe.

Public swimming pools must have a fence or wall around them. This fence must be at least 6 feet (1.8 m) high for below-ground pools. The path around the pool must be at least 4 feet (1.2 m) wide. The shallow end of the pool must be at least 3 feet (0.9 m) deep, but no more than 3 feet 6 inches (1 m) deep.

LET'S EXPLORE MATH

A tiler has been asked to tile the bottom of a pool. The pool is a rectangular shape. It is 25 yards long and has 8 lanes. Each lane is 7 feet wide. A path around the perimeter of the pool is also being laid. *Hint*: 1 yard = 3 feet

a. What is the area of the bottom of the pool in square feet?

b. What is the perimeter of the pool?

A public swimming pool

The plans for public swimming pools must include changing rooms, bathrooms, and showers. Town planners also need to think about how people will get to the pool. They must decide whether the pool needs a parking lot, and whether a bus route should go by the pool.

People line up to enter a public pool in England.

Building Tennis Courts

Many towns have public tennis courts. Tennis courts are shaped like rectangles. It is best to build a tennis court so that it faces north-south (not east-west). That way, the players are less likely to get the sun in their eyes.

Time for Tennis
The first tennis courts were the shape of an **hourglass**. They were narrow in the middle and wider at each end. They were also shorter than tennis courts today.

There are rules about the size of tennis courts. A tennis court must be 78 feet (23.7 m) long. For singles matches, the court needs to be 27 feet (8.2 m) wide. For doubles matches, it needs to be 36 feet (10.9 m) wide.

Singles matches are played between 2 people. Doubles matches are played between 4 people, in 2 teams of 2.

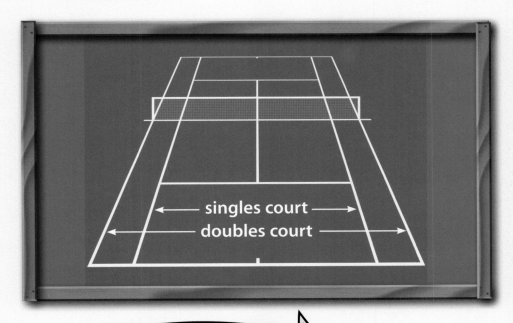

singles court
doubles court

LET'S EXPLORE MATH

For singles matches, the tennis court is 78 feet long and 27 feet wide. For doubles matches, the tennis court is 78 feet long and 36 feet wide. What is the difference between the area of the singles court and the doubles court?

On a tennis court, the net must be 3 feet 6 inches (1.09 m) high at the posts, and 3 feet (0.9 m) high in the center. There must be extra space around the court so players can run to reach the balls. This space is usually between 12 and 24 feet (3.6 and 7.3 m).

In many cities and towns around the world, there are public tennis courts that can be used by all people. Does your neighborhood have public tennis courts?

Building Parks

Towns and cities need to have parks where people can go to relax or play. Parks are carefully designed to meet the needs of the people in the town. Parks can have playgrounds, picnic areas, and even sports fields. Parks need to be planned so that each of these special places can fit within the park.

Hyde Park is a large park in London, England.

Special places within a park must be planned, too. The area of a playground must be measured to check that the equipment will fit inside. The area of a sandbox must be measured so the right amount of sand can be added.

A playground in a park

This park is 280 meters long and 155 meters wide.

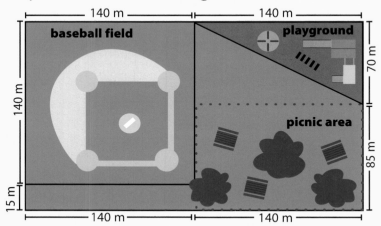

a. What is the perimeter of the park?

b. What is the area of the baseball field?

c. What is the area of the picnic area?

d. What is the area of the playground?

Who Pays?

Roads, swimming pools, tennis courts, and parks all cost the government money. Most of the money comes from the people who live in the town. When workers get paid, part of their **wages** go to the government. This money is called taxes. Some of the taxes paid by the people in a town go toward building these places they can enjoy.

A building site in a town

Growing Towns and Cities

More people around the world are living in cities and towns. As city and town **populations** grow, governments need to make plans for new housing, roads, parks, and other places. These places need to be carefully planned so that they are safe. They should meet the needs of the people who live nearby.

There are about 400,000 miles (644,000 km) of public roads in Germany.

Places like swimming pools, tennis courts, and parks can make life in a town or city better. It is the government's job to make sure these places are the right size and meet all the right standards. Then everybody in a city or town can enjoy them.

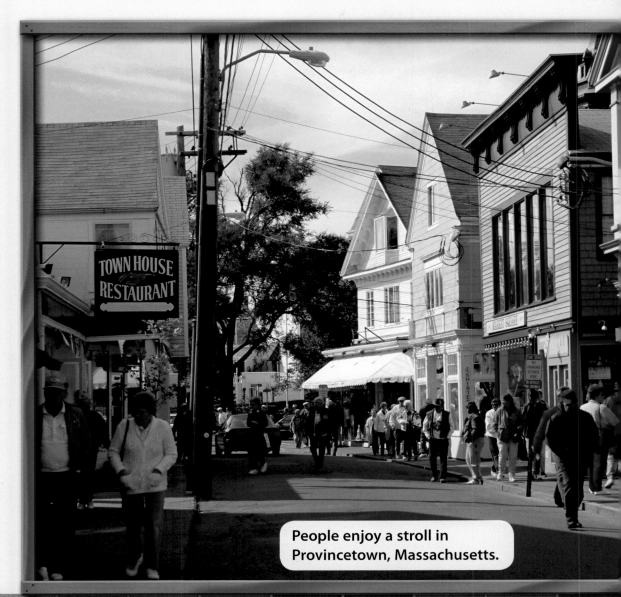

People enjoy a stroll in Provincetown, Massachusetts.

Carnival Fun

Chen and Natasha are planning a school carnival. Below is a plan of where everything can be found at the carnival. On their plan, each small square is 5 yards x 5 yards.

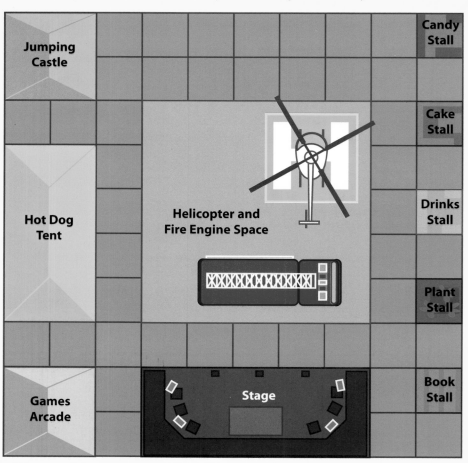

Solve It!

a. The space for the helicopter and fire engine needs to be fenced off with rope. How many yards of rope are needed?

b. Find the dimensions of the stage. Then calculate the area of the stage.

c. Find the total area of the 5 small stalls.

d. Chen and Natasha can fit 4 sets of tables and chairs in 25 square yards. Calculate how many sets of tables and chairs they could fit in half the area of the hot dog tent.

Use the steps below to help you work out your answers.

Step 1: Find the perimeter of the helicopter and fire engine space.

Step 2: Find the length and width of the stage. Then figure out the area.

Step 3: Figure out the area of each of the stalls. Then add the areas.

Step 4: Figure out the area of the hot dog tent. Halve the area. Then figure out how many sets of tables and chairs can fit into that area.

Glossary

accurate—correct

architect—a person who designs and plans new buildings and other structures

area—the space inside a particular shape or place

competitive—relating to or based on competition

dimensions—sizes or measurements

grid—a pattern of vertical and horizontal lines

hourglass—a container used for measuring time that is narrow in the middle and wider at each end

irregular—unusual, not a regular shape

perimeter—the distance around a particular shape or space

permanent—fixed, not temporary

populations—the number of people who live in particular places

standards—rules and regulations

suburbs—the area around a city or town where people live

surveyor—a person who collects, studies, or inspects land measurements

tract—a defined area of land

wages—money received for doing a job

Index

Let's Explore Math

Page 5:

a. Area: 4 square miles (4 mi.^{2})
Perimeter: $2 + 2 + 2 + 2 = 8$ miles

b. Area: 6 square miles (6 mi.^{2})
Perimeter: $3 + 2 + 3 + 2 = 10$ miles

c. Perimeter: $3 + 3 + 3 + 3 = 12$ miles

Page 7:

a. Area: 112 square miles (112 mi.^{2})
Perimeter: $14 + 8 + 14 + 8 = 44$ miles

b. Answers will vary. Sample Answers:
Richmond could be any of the
following: 9 miles long and 5 miles
wide; 5 miles long and 9 miles wide;
15 miles long and 3 miles wide;
3 miles long and 15 miles wide

Page 9:

a. and **b.**

Lot	Area	Perimeter
A	6,000 ft.^{2}	340 ft.
B	8,400 ft.^{2}	380 ft.
C	7,800 ft.^{2}	370 ft.
D	6,600 ft.^{2}	350 ft.

c. Answers will vary.

Page 11:
Area $= \frac{1}{2} \times 80$ ft. $\times 50$ ft. $= 2,000$ ft.^{2}

Page 12:

a. 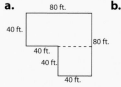 **b.**

a. 40 ft. $\times$ 80 ft. $= 3,200$ ft.^{2}
40 ft. $\times$ 40 ft. $= 1,600$ ft.^{2}
3,200 ft.^{2} $+$ 1,600 ft.^{2} $= 4,800$ ft.^{2}

b. $\frac{1}{2} \times 40$ ft. $\times 40$ ft. $= 800$ ft.^{2}
3,200 ft.^{2} $+$ 800 ft.^{2} $= 4,000$ ft.^{2}

Page 15:

a. Area: 14 ft. $\times$ 12 ft. $= 168$ ft.^{2}

b. 168 ft.^{2} $\times$ 5 bricks $= 840$ bricks

c. Answers will vary.

Page 18:

a. Length: 25 yards $\times$ 3 $= 75$ feet
Width: 8 lanes $\times$ 7 feet $= 56$ feet
Area: 75 ft. $\times$ 56 ft. $= 4,200$ ft.^{2}

b. Perimeter: 75 ft. $+$ 56 ft. $+$ 75 ft. $+$ 56 ft. $= 262$ ft.

Page 21:
Area of singles court: 78 ft. $\times$ 27 ft. $= 2,106$ ft.^{2}
Area of doubles court: 78 ft. $\times$ 36 ft. $= 2,808$ ft.^{2}
Difference: 2,808 ft.^{2} $-$ 2,106 ft.^{2} $= 702$ ft.^{2}

Page 24:

a. Perimeter: 280 m $+$ 155 m $+$ 280 m $+$ 155 m
$= 870$ meters

b. Area: 140 m $\times$ 140 m $= 19,600$ m^2

c. Area: 85 m $\times$ 140 m $= 11,900$ m^2

d. Area: $\frac{1}{2}$ of 140 m $= 70$ m; 70 m $\times$ 70 m
$= 4,900$ m^2 or $\frac{1}{2}$ of 70 m $= 35$ m;
35 m $\times$ 140 m $= 4,900$ m^2

Problem-Solving Activity

a. Perimeter of helicopter and fire engine
space: 25 yds. $\times$ 4 $= 100$ yds.

b. Stage dimensions: 25 yds. long and
10 yds. wide.
Area of stage: 25 yds. $\times$ 10 yds. $= 250$ yds.^{2}

c. Total area: 25 yds.^{2} $+$ 25 yds.^{2} $+$ 25 yds.^{2}
$+$ 25 yds.^{2} $+$ 25 yds.^{2} $= 125$ yds.^{2}

d. Area $= 20$ yds. $\times$ 10 yds. $= 200$ yds.^{2}
$\frac{1}{2}$ of 200 yds.^{2} $= 100$ yds.^{2}
100 yds.^{2} $\div$ 25 yds.^{2} $= 4$
4 sets of tables and chairs $\times$ 4 $= 16$ sets of
tables and chairs